In This Bedroom

Nancy Harris

www.raintreepublishers.co.uk
Visit our website to find out more information about Raintree books.

To order:
☎ Phone +44 (0) 1865 888066
▤ Fax +44 (0) 1865 314091
▣ Visit www.raintreepublishers.co.uk

Raintree is an imprint of Capstone Global Library Limited, a company incorporated in England and Wales having its registered office at 7 Pilgrim Street, London, EC4V 6LB – Registered company number: 6695582

"Raintree" is a registered trademark of Pearson Education Limited, under licence to Capstone Global Library Limited

Edited by Rebecca Rissman, Nancy Dickmann, and Sian Smith
Designed by Joanna Hinton-Malivoire
Original illustrations © Capstone Global Library Ltd., 2010
Illustrated by Kevin Rechin
Picture research by Tracy Cummins
Originated by Capstone Global Library Ltd
Printed and bound in China by Leo Paper Products Ltd

ISBN 978 140621316 4 (hardback)
14 13 12 11 10
10 9 8 7 6 5 4 3 2 1

British Library Cataloguing in Publication Data
Harris, Nancy.
What's lurking in this house?.
In this bedroom.
1. Household pests--Juvenile literature. 2. Microbial ecology--Juvenile literature. 3. Bedrooms--Juvenile literature.
I. Title
579.1'7-dc22

Acknowledgements
The author and publisher are grateful to the following for permission to reproduce copyright material: Alamy pp.**16**, **18** (© Nigel Cattlin), **27** (© Nikki Edmunds); Bugwood. org p.**17** (© Clemson University - USDA Cooperative Extension Slide Series); Getty Images pp.**7** bottom (Nigel Cattlin), **10** (Dag Sundberg), **15** (John Downer); Photo Researchers, Inc. pp.**7 centre** (© Andrew Syred), **9** (© Eye of Science), **12** (© Andrew Syred), **21** (©Kenneth Eward), **23** (© David M. Phillips), **25** (© Julie Dermansky); Photolibrary p.**26** (Marc Gilsdorf); Shutterstock pp. **7 top** (© 6493866629), **8** (© Oberon), **13** (© Chris Rodenberg Photography), **20** (© Evok20), **29 bedbug** (© Artur Tiutenko), **29 mould** (© Robert Adrian Hillman), **29 office** (© terekhov igor); SuperStock p.**28** (Brand X). Cover photograph of bedbugs reproduced with permission of Science Photo Library (Eye of Science).

Every effort has been made to contact copyright holders of any material reproduced in this book. Any omissions will be rectified in subsequent printings if notice is given to the publisher.

All the Internet addresses (URLs) given in this book were valid at the time of going to press. However, due to the dynamic nature of the Internet, some addresses may have changed, or sites may have changed or ceased to exist since publication. While the author and publisher regret any inconvenience this may cause readers, no responsibility for any such changes can be accepted by either the author or the publisher.

Some words are shown in bold, **like this**. You can find out what they mean by looking in the glossary.

Contents

Is something lurking in this house?

A house is a place where you eat, sleep, work, and play. You sleep and sometimes work or play in the bedroom. But do you ever think about what may be living in your bedroom?

Bedtime

It's bedtime. You lie down on your bed, rest your head on the pillow, and pull up the covers. You turn off the light. It is just you and your bed in the dark. Or is it? What else is lurking in your bedroom?

? Find out what these
things are later on …

Tiny crawlers

As you sleep, very tiny bugs called dust mites move around your bedroom. They are so small you need to use a **microscope** to see them.

Dust mites often live in mattresses and carpets.

microscope

A magnified dust mite.

flake of
dead skin

FUN FACT

We lose pieces of dead skin
all the time. This is what dust
mites love to eat!

10   Do you dribble when you sleep?

Dust mites like to live in warm places. They also like to be near wet or **moist** places. This is why they live in your mattress and pillow. Your body's heat and sweat keeps them warm and damp. So does your dribble.

Blood-sucking bedbugs

Some unlucky people have bedbugs living in their bedrooms. You don't need a **microscope** to spot bedbugs. They are about the size of an apple seed.

bedbug

Bedbugs can hide in your bed or even on cuddly toys.

Bedbugs usually come out and eat at night. They are **parasites**. This means they feed on other animals. They bite people as they sleep and drink their blood.

bedbug

Tasty jumpers

Have you ever spotted a hole in one of your jumpers? It could have been eaten by a young clothes moth. Young clothes moths are called **larvae**. They are white and look like caterpillars.

clothes moth larva

FUN FACT

Adult clothes moths can be white, grey, or brown. They can be about a centimetre long. That is about the same length as a sunflower seed.

adult clothes moth

case

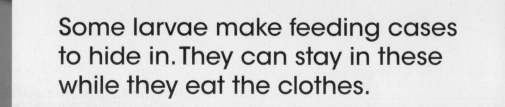

Some larvae make feeding cases to hide in. They can stay in these while they eat the clothes.

Clothes moths **larvae**, or young, like to eat wool, hair, and feathers. They like to eat in dark and quiet places. Your wardrobe is a great place for these insects to eat. It is dark and full of tasty things to munch on.

Germ busting

Many other things live in your bedroom. **Germs** are another thing to watch out for. Germs are very small living things that can cause illness. You need to use a **microscope** to see germs.

FUN FACT

One of the main places you can find germs is on your mattress and bedding. Change your sheets often!

This is an enlarged picture of germs.

germs that cause colds

Hungry bacteria

Bacteria are a type of **germ**. You can only see bacteria under a **microscope**. Bacteria can be found almost anywhere. They are on your pillow, mattress, and clothing. Some bacteria can make you ill.

FUN FACT

Bacteria can even be found on your alarm clock button!

Bacteria are not fussy eaters. They eat the dead skin that can be found all over a bedroom.

bacteria

skin

Growing in the corner

Mould is a small living thing. Mould likes to live in warm places. Mould can only live in wet or **moist** places. Your bedroom can be moist and warm.

mould

mould

Mould can make you ill. Look out for mould in your bedroom!

You could see blue mould on your carpet. You could see white mould on your wallpaper. You could see black mould on your ceiling. EEEK!

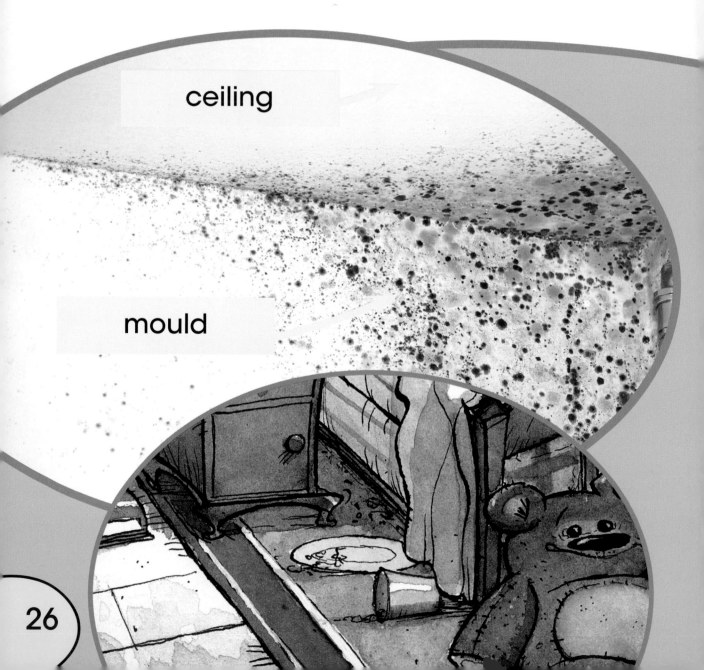

ceiling

mould

This mould is growing in a cup of old drink!

FUN FACT

Mould can grow in many places. It can be many colours.

Keeping it clean

You never know what might be lurking in your bedroom. Vacuum your carpets and floor. Wash your clothes and sheets. This will help to reduce the amount of creatures and **germs** in your bedroom.

Fun facts

The average desk has more than 10,000 germs living on it.

Bedbugs die at high temperatures. Putting bedding in a tumble dryer kills them off.

Bedbugs have a flat shape. This helps them to hide in narrow spaces.

There are about 150 different types of house mould.

Approximately three dust mites can fit into the full stop at the end of this sentence.

Glossary

bacteria tiny living things. Bacteria are a type of germ.

germs tiny living things that can make you ill if they get inside your body

larvae the young of some types of insect

microscope instrument used to see very small things, such as germs

moist wet or damp

parasites living things that feed on other living things

Find out more

Find out

Why can't people feel bedbug bites?

Books

Awesome Bugs: Butterflies and Moths, Anna Claybourne (Franklin Watts, 2004)

Germs, Ross Collins (Bloomsbury Publishing, 2005)

Parasites: Bedbugs, Shelley Bueche (KidHaven Press, 2005)

Where to Find Minibeasts: Minibeasts in the Home, Sarah Ridley (Smart Apple Media, 2009)

Websites

http://kidshealth.org/kid/talk/qa/germs.html
This section on the Kid's Health website tells you about germs and how to protect yourself from them.

http://pestworldforkids.org/bedbugs.html
Learn about bedbugs on this website. Find out how to keep them out of your home.

http://www.pestworldforkids.org/dust-mites.html
This website tells you about dust mites. It includes information on what they eat and where they live.

Index